NATIVE AMERICAN

Native American Essential Oils and remedies to be
in perfect shape without drugs

Lily jones

Contents

Instructions:

Put everything save the beeswax into a saucepan, give it a good stir, and then put it on low heat for anything between six and twelve hours. The oil and the herbs will combine in the proper manner, and the oil will become infused with the medicinal properties of the herb extracts as a result.

Begin by melting the beeswax in a double boiler over low heat. Next, pass the oil through a cheesecloth filter before adding it to the melting beeswax. It needs to be twisted and squeezed firmly enough to help every last drop of oil find its way into the bowl.

The remaining debris should be removed from the cheesecloth, and then thrown away. After meticulously combining the wax and oil to get a mixture that is uniform throughout, turn off the boiler.

To get rid of a diaper rash, take one teaspoon of this ointment and carefully spread it on the affected area. This should be done multiple times each day.

Place in a cool and dry storage area.

2. Diaper Rash Gel with Echinacea and Chamomile

Ingredients:

1/4 cup aloe vera gel

1 tablespoon dried chamomile

Half-cup water

1 tablespoon dried Echinacea herb

Instructions:

Cook for at least six to twelve hours, stirring occasionally, ensuring that none of the ingredients burn. The water and the herbs will appropriately blend, and the medicinal benefits of the herb extracts will be absorbed by the water.

Before pouring the liquid into the jar, first drain it through some cheesecloth into the jar. It should be twisted and pressed firmly enough to ensure that each and every drop of the extract is transferred into the dish.

The remaining debris should be removed from the cheesecloth, and then thrown away. After thoroughly combining the aloe vera gel and extract in a separate bowl with caution, turn off the boiler and set the mixture aside.

Apply this gel to the affected region, and then gently massage it into the skin until it is fully absorbed.

Place in a cool and dry storage area.

5.1.2 Chickenpox

The itchy sickness known as chickenpox is characterized by little lesions that look like poxes and spread across the entire body's surface skin. Ninety percent of children will get it at an early age, indicating that it is highly prevalent among children. However, if you've already had chickenpox, there's a good chance you won't get it again in your lifetime.

1. Calendula and Goldenseal gel for Chicken Pox

Ingredients:

1 and a half cup aloe vera gel

1 ounce dried calendula herb

2 glasses water

1 ounce dried goldenseal root

Instructions:

Combine all of the ingredients, with the exception of the aloe Vera gel, in a pan, give it a good stir, and then put it on low heat for anywhere between six and twelve hours. The water and the herbs will appropriately blend, and the medicinal benefits of the herb extracts will be absorbed by the water.

Before pouring the liquid into the jar, first drain it through some cheesecloth into the jar. It should be twisted and pressed firmly enough to ensure that each and every drop of the extract is transferred into the dish.

The remaining debris should be removed from the cheesecloth, and then thrown away. After thoroughly combining the aloe vera gel and extract in a separate bowl with caution, turn off the boiler and set the mixture aside.

If you want to seek treatment for chickenpox, apply this gel to the affected region in a gentle manner.

Place in a cool and dry storage area.

2. Body Bath Made from Licorice and Comfrey for Chickenpox

Ingredients:

Licorice root tincture (half teaspoon)

4 cups apple cider vinegar, unfiltered and organic

Comfrey herbs, half tsp. tincture

Instructions:

Combine the vinegar and tinctures in a clean, dry container.

It's ready to use if you keep it in a dark, dry place.

See remarkable results by mixing one cup of the prepared mixture with one cup of water.

5.1.3 Throat Infection

Children are more likely to get sore throats due to their lack of awareness and the fact that they frequently ingest cold meals and beverages. In addition, children and adolescents typically have compromised immune systems, which contributes to the prevalence of conditions of this kind.

1. For a Sore Throat, Gargle with Licorice and Agrimony

Ingredients:

1 teaspoon crushed licorice

1 cup water

1 tsp. natural honey

1 tablespoon dried agrimony herbs

Instructions:

Boil the water, and then add the rest of the ingredients.

For a few minutes, keep it covered.

One tbsp. is all you'll need. Then, gargle with the concoction, and your youngster will feel much better.

2. Sore Throat Tea with Sage, Peppermint, and Comfrey

Ingredients:

1 teaspoon dried comfrey

1 teaspoon dried peppermint

1 tsp. sage (dried form)

1 cup water

Ingredients:

Fill a cup halfway with water that has been brought to a boil.

Place the sage, peppermint, and comfrey herbs in the cup and cover with a lid for a few minutes.

Drink the tea after a while, when the herbs have nicely mingled in the water.

This tea should be consumed three to four times a day to treat your child's sore throat.

5.1.4 Colic Illness

Newborns and infants between the ages of two and four months might suffer from colic, which is an unpleasant sickness. The most common symptoms include extended bouts of weeping, an inability to sleep, and an agitated state of mind. Herbal remedies will not be able to prevent the discomfort caused by colic because there are many causes; nonetheless, they will assist reduce the pain.

1. Colic Treatment Using Herbal Gripe Water

Ingredients:

1 teaspoon dried peppermint leaves, crushed

1 teaspoon fennel seeds, crushed

1 teaspoon sugar made from cane

1 teaspoon fresh ginger root, diced

1 cup hot water

Instructions:

In a mug, combine the herbs and water.

Bring the water to a boil and pour it into the mug.

Allow the herbs to soak in the mug after covering it with a lid.

Fill a sterile jar with the substance and use it.

You can use a dropper to give it to your child and have him or her take it orally.

Your child will feel relieved in no time.

To get the best results, take the drug twice a day.

2. The Use of Chamomile Infusion in the Treatment of Colic

Ingredients:

One teaspoon dried chamomile

1 cup water

Instructions:

Fill a cup halfway with water that has been brought to a boil.

Place the peppermint and fennel herbs in the cup and cover with a lid for a few minutes.

Drink the tea after a while, when the herbs have nicely mingled in the water.

This tea should be consumed three to four times a day to cure your child's colic problem.

5.1.5 Ear Infection

The most typical reason for earache or pain in the ear is an infection. It is fairly common among children, and the associated discomfort can be brutally agonizing for the child.

1. Mullein and Garlic Infused Oil for Ear Pain

Ingredients:

2 tbsp. olive oil (mild)

1 ounce dried mullein

2 tsp. garlic (dry form)

Instructions:

Put all of the ingredients into a saucepan, then set the saucepan on a double boiler that's half full of water, and stir the mixture frequently. Cook for a minimum of three and up to five hours. Because the water and the herbs will properly combine, the herbal extracts will be able to seep into the oil and deliver the desired therapeutic benefits.

Before pouring the liquid into the jar, first drain it through some cheesecloth into the jar. It should be twisted and pressed firmly enough to ensure that each and every drop of the extract is transferred into the dish.

The remaining debris should be removed from the cheesecloth, and then thrown away.

Put two or three drops of this oil into your child's ear, and you should feel some relief from the discomfort it's causing.

kept in a cool, dry area for storage.

2. Poultice made from Blue Vervain for Ear Pain

Ingredients:

1 cup water

2 teaspoons dried blue vervain

Instructions:

To start, bring the water to a boil in the saucepan.

After adding the herbs, wait a few minutes with the lid on the pan.

A cheesecloth should be used to strain the infused water into a mug.

Now, take a cotton swab and soak it in the poultice before rubbing it on your child's ear. This should be done several times.

You should be prepared for impacts that deviate significantly from the norm.

If you are interested in giving your child a herbal medicine, you should first discuss your plans with your family physician and then speak with an experienced herbalist about how to administer the treatment and what dosage they recommend. Children's sensitivity to herbs, like sensitivities to any other drug, can differ from adults' sensitivities, thus act with extreme caution when administering herbal therapies to children.

Chapter 1

Native Americans made extensive use of several essential oils.

An strong hydrophobic liquid that is recognized for containing volatile chemical components derived from plants is referred to as an essential oil. Essential oils can also be referred to as volatile oils, petroleum, ethereal oils, or simply the plant soil from which they were derived by flowers, roots, leaves, wood, bars, seeds, or peels. All of these terms refer to the same thing. Essential oil is essential in the sense that it has the "essence of" the plant's scent, the distinctive scent of the herb or plant from which it was extracted. Aromatherapy was used in ancient ceremonies to combat pessimism and evil. Our ancestors believed that good scents fend off evil spirits and keep wicked creatures at a distance.

1.1 The Development of Essential Oils

Essential oils have been used throughout history in many forms of traditional medicine. It is believed that Ibn al-Baitar, an Arabic Spanish Muslim general practitioner, chemist, and pharmacist, was the first to mention the techniques and methods that are used to produce essential oils. Ibn Sina, a Persian surgeon also known as Avicenna in Europe, was the first to originate the Attar or scent of flowers from the distillation method. Avicenna was the first to bring this discovery to Europe. In many recent articles, essential oils are discussed in terms of the individual chemical compounds that make them up. For example, "wintergreen oil" is more likely to be referred to as methyl salicylate than methyl salicylate alone. In the most recent decades, there has been a resurgence in interest in herbal essential oils due to the advent of aromatherapy. Aromatherapy is a form of alternative medicine that makes use of herbal oils in addition to other fragrant compounds. Volatilized oils are utilized in massage, dispersed in the atmosphere using a nebulizer or diffuser, burned as incense, and the candle flame was used to heat it.

1.2 Aromatherapy practiced by Native Americans and their contributions

Native Americans and other ancient civilizations have, for a very long time, incorporated the use of the herbal oils into their daily routines as well as their spiritual and domestic rituals. They have a profound respect for Mother Nature, and as a result, they opt to solely use natural items in their day-to-day life. They believe that the powerful aromas of the herbal oils can fend off evil spirits while also boosting their overall health, and this is why they use them. For instance, cleansing ceremonies practiced by Native Americans make use of aromatic oils and various herbs. Aromatic herbs like Sage, Sweetgrass, Cedarwood, Juniper, Pine

Opinion Spikes, and others help purify the air, get rid of negative energies, and appeal to bring more optimism into life. But why would we even talk about aromatherapy when it comes to the Native American tradition? It is easy, useful, fundamental, and has a really natural feel to it. Aromatherapists in the United States have a deeper understanding of aromatherapy than aromatherapists in other countries; as a result, they are aware of which essential oils and plants can be used to counteract negative energy in the form of intense emotions, mental turmoil, and other forms. The vast majority of the herbs and oils used by the Natives may be found almost anywhere, including online and at specialty aromatherapy stores. They use the herbs in their most unadulterated and natural state, as fragrant plants with aromas, rather than constructing pleasing mixtures of the herbs (as many aromatherapists do).

1.3 Native Americans commonly use smudging as a spiritual practice.

Smudging is a sacred custom among American Indians that consists of burning plants for the purpose of purification and prayer. The vast majority of American Indians participate in this activity. In addition, the combustion of the herbs releases a variety of enticing aromas that are derived from the plant's essential oils, which further enhances the overall experience. Following this, the smoke produced by the herbs is utilized in the performance of religious rites. During a smudging ceremony, people pray aloud to the Creator while passing a bundle of burning herbs from one person to the next. Smudging is considered to be a spiritually healing practice. Two plants frequently used for smudging are sweetgrass and sage. Other plants that can be used for smudging include bergamot, yarrow, mesquite, bearberry, and tobacco. These herbs can be used on their own or combined with others. It is believed that prayers and laments would be carried up to the spirits in spiritual rites by the smoke that is produced when sage and sweetgrass are burned. The majority of the time, the medical applications presented by those selling medicinal oils range from skin care therapies to cancer treatments, and they are frequently based simply on historical records of the use of essential oils for these purposes. Claims made regarding the effectiveness of medical therapies, notably cancer treatment, are now regulated in the majority of countries throughout the world.

Chapter 2

How to Prepare Essential Oils and How Do They Work?

2 .1 Methods of Preparation for Essential Oils

Essential oils are liquid extracts that can be derived from a wide range of plants and have the potential to have a variety of applications. Manufacturing processes can be used to successfully extract the important chemicals that these plants contain. Essential oils have a more potent aroma and are packed with more of the active compounds that are found in the plants that they are distilled from. Because so much plant material is required in order to extract the essential oil, this is the case. The following are some of the methods that are used by producers to extract essential oils:

2.1.1 Distillation with either Water or Steam

The plants are put through a process in which water or hot steam is sent through them, which separates the vital components from the plant debris.

2.1.2 Pressing with Cold

Mechanically pressing or squeezing plant matter to liberate important juices or oils is how this technique works. Smelling the fresh perfume of lemon after squeezing or zesting a Lemon peel is a simple illustration of this.

2.1.3 Extraction using Solvents

The majority of flowers have chemical components that are too delicate to be destroyed by the high heat required in steam distillation, but they also contain too little volatile oil to be extracted and utilised. As an alternative, the oils are extracted with the help of a solvent such as supercritical or hexane, or even CO_2.

Concretes are a mixture of essential herbal oil, resins, waxes, and other oil-soluble (lipophilic) plant material that has been significantly extracted from hexane and hydrophobic additional solvents. Even though they have a strong aroma, concretes include a large amount of waxes and resins that are not aromatic. It is common practice to use another solvent, such as ethyl alcohol, in order to extract the fragrant oil from the concrete. When the alcohol solution is kept at a temperature of 0 degrees Fahrenheit (18 degrees Celsius) for longer than 48 hours, waxes and lipids begin to precipitate out of solution. After that, the precipitates are removed using a filter, and the ethanol that was in the solution that was left behind is removed using either a vacuum purge or evaporation, or both of these methods, leaving the absolute. As a common solvent, supercritical carbon dioxide is frequently utilized in the process of extracting supercritical fluids. Unlike steam distillation, this method does not leave petrochemical residues in the final product, but it does result in the loss of some "top notes." However, this does not directly result in the production of an absolute. The use of supercritical carbon dioxide will be employed in order to obtain the essential oils and waxes contained in the concrete. The use of further processing with liquefied carbon dioxide is required in order to separate the waxes from the essential oils. This additional processing can be achieved in the same extractor by lowering the extraction temperature. Because of the lower temperature involved in this process, compounds do not break down or become denaturized. When the extraction process is complete, the pressure is lowered to the normal level, and the carbon dioxide reverts back into a gas without leaving any residue.

2.1.4 Getting Your Hands on Florals

Floral 134a is an additional solvent that can be utilized in the process of extracting essential oils. It was developed to serve as an alternative to Freon in its capacity as a refrigerant. Despite being a chemical that is considered to be "ozone-friendly," floral has a high global warming potential (GWP; 100-year GWP = 1430). As a direct consequence of this, the European Union has made its use illegal, with a phase-out period beginning in 2011 and continuing through 2017.

Floral has the advantage of being able to extract essential oils at room temperature or lower, preventing deterioration that can be caused by high temperatures. The essential oils are mostly unadulterated and only contain a trace amount of impurities. In order to extract more product from the same quantity of essential oil, some manufacturers would blend the active compounds that are derived from plant matter with a carrier or base oil. Because of this, these oils would no longer be considered pure essential oils but rather a combination.

2.2 How Do Essential Oils Actually Work?

The most common application of essential oils is in the practice of aromatherapy, which involves inhaling the vapors of the oils in a variety of ways. The essential oils are never meant to be swallowed. Essential oils include molecules or particles that interact with your body in a variety of different ways, depending on the oil.

When they are placed on the skin, certain plant composites can be absorbed. It is believed that some application methods, such as applying the substance with heat or to multiple regions of the body, increase the rate of absorption. Despite this, there is not a lot of research in this area. The limbic system, which is involved in actions, emotions, and long-term memory, can be triggered by essential oil fragrances. This system is also involved in the sense of smell. Unexpectedly, the limbic system is responsible for a significant portion of the development of memories. Therefore, it might be helpful to describe why specific odors might stimulate emotions or memories in a person.

A number of involuntary physiological processes, such as blood respiration, heart rate, and pressure, are all under the direction of the limbic system in the brain. Because of this, it is generally accepted that essential oils have a palpable effect on the human body. After being diluted, essential oils can either be inhaled or used topically to the skin. It's possible that ingesting them will heighten your sense of smell or give you medicinal benefits.

2.3 How Should You Make Use of Essential Oils?

2.3.1 Use Diffuser

Use a vaporizer that is water-based.

Use 1–2 drops of essential oil in a diffuser and run it for 10 minutes before turning it off for another 30 minutes.

Place the diffuser away from the pet's reach, such as on a high shelf or in a room corner.

2.3.2 Room Spray

Excessive exposure to oils should be avoided.

Spraying on pillows, other fabrics, toys, and items is not a good idea.

It aids in the creation of a relaxing environment.

2.3.3 Topical Application

Always use Carrier Oil to dilute.

Add essential oils in shampoos, locations, soaps, and moisturizing creams or massage on the body. Because essential oils are concentrated in nature, they should not be applied directly to the skin. This is because it has the potential to cause skin irritation.

2.4 Three Aroma Notes Of Essential Oil

It is also possible to discriminate between the "notes" that are most prominent in each scent family. For instance, the "note" of the essential oil's aroma is what defines how long the perfume will last on the wearer. The three sorts of notes that can be played are the top, middle, and base notes. However, the majority of oils only have a single, distinguishable note that predominates the others, giving them a rich, full-bodied, and luxurious appearance. The presence of multiple notes in some oils gives them these qualities. Because the Essential Oils that are contained in an oil blend all have varying degrees of volatility, which means that they have varying rates of evaporation, the scent of an oil blend will change over time, even over a short period of time, such as from morning to afternoon. The reason for this is that the evaporation of each oil at its own rate is what causes the scent to change. Even over a short period of time, such as from morning to afternoon. The essential oils that have the smallest molecules and are therefore the most volatile are the first to evaporate when combined with other essential oils. The top note oils are the first to be detected, but they are also the first to go. The oils that contain the largest and, as a result, the heaviest molecules also dissipate the slowly or last, which results in longer scents. Notes from the Base series can be found here. The Top and Base notes are combined with the Middle notes, which are made up of Essential Oils that release their scents in stages and provide a more balanced aroma.

2.5 How Can I Make an Essential Oil Blend That Is Perfectly Balanced in Its Components?

The simplest technique to make a well-rounded oil blend is to limit yourself to no more than five essential oils:

Base note oil

Middle note oils

Top note oil

There are no precise standards for which oils should or should not be used when creating Essential Oil blends; however, the following standard can serve as a guiding concept to help support a congruent mixture, especially when starting:

For one drop of a Base note,

Add two drops of Middle notes

And three drops of Top notes

Alternately, you might combine each essential oil by adding one drop at a time until you reach the desired aroma. When creating new combinations, the total amount of all of the combined essential oils should be no more than 5 drops, and no less than 25 drops. The Low and Middle tones should be mixed together initially. After you have achieved the desired aroma with this combination, proceed to add the Top note. Continue adding one drop of each type of oil at a time until the correct mixture is achieved or the maximum number of droplets is reached.

It is helpful to write notes with each addition in order to keep track of the oils and the amounts that they each contribute. Before using the finished mixture, let it "rest" for twenty-four hours so that the aroma has a chance to fully emerge. Before beginning the production of any mixes or putting them into use, check to see that all of the safety procedures are followed. Before applying the mixture directly to the skin, it should first be diluted with a Carrier Oil.

2.6 Oils

The aromatic leaves, bark, and roots of plants are utilized in the production of essential oils. However, when they are applied to the skin directly, they have the potential to produce considerable irritation as well as redness and burning. Carrier oils are used to dilute essential oils and assist in "carrying" the essential oils into the skin. Sometimes, odorless body lotion or gels made from aloe vera are used as a carrier rather than water. Carrier oils are vegetable oils that are produced from the nuts, seeds, or kernels of a plant. Some examples of carrier oils include avocado oil and coconut oil. When producing the oil for use in aromatherapy, cold pressing is the method that should be used. Crushing the plants in this manner results in the extraction of the oil. Users assert, on the other hand, that heating the oil during extraction destroys the delicate elements of the oil. The majority of carrier oils have a faint scent that can be described as sweet and nutty, however some are odorless. This is because, unlike essential oils, they do not vanish into thin air.

2.6.1 Best Carrier Oils

Carrier oils differ in their characteristics and applications. The intended consequence will determine the carrier oil for aromatherapy.

Coconut Oil

Jojoba Oil

Avocado Oil

Castor Oil

Black cumin seed Oil

Grapeseed Oil

Rosehip Oil

Rosehip Oil

Sweet Almond Oil

Extra Virgin Olive Oil

Sunflower Seed Oil

Safflower Oil

Argan Oil

Hemp Seed Oil

These mineral-rich carrier oils are known to reduce inflammation, fight germs, and inhibit fungal growth. Aromatherapy is a complementary therapy that involves the application of a variety of essential oils to different parts of the body in order to promote overall health on both the physical and mental levels. Aromatherapy makes use of carrier oils in its practice. Carrier oils are used to dilute more potent essential oils, making it possible to apply them to the skin without causing irritation. Aromatherapy is effective in treating a wide range of conditions, such as acne, asthma, depression, insomnia, migraines, and even worms. In order to produce massage and body oils, essential oils are mixed with one or more carrier oils.

2.7 How Do I Determine Which Essential Oils Will Work Best for Me?

There is a large number of businesses that sell their oils as being "pure" or of "medical grade." These concepts, on the other hand, are devoid of any relevance because there is no general agreement over how they should be defined. The production of essential oils is a relatively unregulated sector; as a result, the quality and composition of various essential oils can differ substantially from one another. Only oils that have had their plant components cold-pressed or distilled are used in the production of oils of the highest grade. This is done in order to preserve the integrity of the plant components. It is in your best interest to steer clear of utilizing oils that have been cut with artificial fragrances, chemicals, or other oils. Choosing oils of the best quality will be much easier if you keep the following things in mind while shopping:

You should look for an oil that does not contain any additives or synthetic oils; instead, it should have just the aromatic molecules that can be found in plants. As opposed to words like "essential oil of lavender," the botanical name of the plant will often be identified on pure oils (such as Lavandula officinalis).

When compared to the production of any other kind of oil, the extraction procedure alters real essential oils the least. This holds true regardless of the type of oil. Choose an essential oil that has been created in a way that does not include the use of any chemicals, such as via mechanical cold pressing or distillation. This is the best approach to ensure that the oil is free of any harmful toxins.

Invest in a company that has established a strong reputation for itself by providing goods that are reliably up to the required quality.

Chapter 3

The Benefits and RiskS of Using Essential Oils

3.1 Benefits of Essential Oils

Essential oils are widely used, yet surprisingly little research has been done on their potential to treat specific diseases. The following is an examination of the research that supports the use of aromatherapy and essential oils to treat a variety of the most prevalent health problems.

3.1.1 Stress and Anxiety

It is anticipated that 43% of people who suffer from stress and anxiety will engage in non-traditional therapy in order to assist them in coping with the symptoms of their conditions. Initial investigations into aromatherapy have shown some promising findings. In addition to conventional treatment, the aroma of certain essential oils has been shown in a number of trials to be effective in the treatment of stress and anxiety. Unfortunately, blinded trials are difficult to conduct due to the scents of the compounds, and it is impossible to rule out biases when they do occur. As a consequence of this, a great number of investigations on the effects of herbal oils to relieve stress and anxiety have come to a disappointing conclusion. Even though the beneficial effects of using essential oils during a rubbing and massage, for example, may only last for the duration of the session, they may still be effective in reducing stress. It was discovered that aromatherapy is also helpful in the treatment of anxiety.

3.1.2 Kill Bacteria

Native plant extracts are antibacterial, therefore they could have been of value to Native Americans as a potential treatment for a variety of ailments. It is possible that medical treatments involving white sage, black sage, or sagebrush could be effective against bacterial infections. In addition, the individual components of these essential oils might prove useful in the research and development of innovative medical treatments that could ultimately save people's lives.

3.1.3 Conditions like Migraines and Headaches are Examples of This

When applied to the forehead and temples, a combination of ethanol and peppermint oil was found to be effective in reducing the intensity of headache pain in two limited trials that were carried out in the 1990s. Recent studies have found that rubbing peppermint and lavender oil onto the skin can help alleviate headache discomfort. In addition, a mixture of chamomile essential oil and sesame oil that is applied to the temples has been suggested as a treatment for headaches and migraines. This is a common treatment for headaches in Persian culture. However, there needs to be a great deal more research done.

3.1.4 Sleep or Insomnia

It has been established that the use of lavender oil can improve the quality of sleep in women after delivery as well as in patients with heart disease. A total of fifteen research on the effects of essential oils on sleep were analyzed, and the results were looked at. The vast majority of studies concluded that breathing essential oils, particularly lavender oil, led to better sleep patterns.

3.1.5 Efforts Made to Reduce the Level of Inflammation

The use of essential oils has been suggested as a potential therapeutic assistance in the battle against inflammatory illnesses. According to the findings of certain studies conducted using test tubes, they have qualities that can reduce inflammation. In a study conducted on mice, administration of a combination of essential oils derived from oregano and thyme was found to be effective in inducing remission from colitis. In two separate tests with rats, the effects of applying oil made from caraway and rosemary were comparable. However, there have only been a handful of human studies that have looked into the benefits that these oils have on inflammatory conditions. As a direct consequence of this, both their usefulness and their safety have not been determined.

3.1.6 Antibiotics and Antimicrobials

The resurgence of infectious diseases caused by bacteria that are resistant to antibiotic treatment has sparked renewed interest in the search for alternative treatments. Essential oils such as tea tree oil and peppermint oil have been subjected to exhaustive research in test tubes to determine the extent of their antibacterial activity, with some encouraging results. The results of these experiments conducted in test tubes are exciting; nevertheless, they do not always reflect how these oils will actually behave in your body. For instance, they do not demonstrate that a particular essential oil can cure microbiological illnesses that are found in people. The use of essential oils has been linked to a variety of potential health advantages. However, additional research on humans is necessary.

3.1.7 Pesticide

Essential oils can work as a natural pesticide. Case studies have shown that some oils have a variety of effects that discourage pests, particularly insects and specific arthropods, from causing damage to a property. Insects and other vermin that consume the oil run the risk of being repelled, having their digestion slowed, their growth stunted, their reproductive rate hindered, or even dying as a result of these repercussions. On the other hand, the compounds found in essential oils that are responsible for inducing these effects are generally safe for animals to consume. Because of the one-of-a-kind responses that the chemicals have, these environmentally friendly insecticides can be used extensively without causing any harm to anything other than the bugs themselves. A number of different essential oils, including rose, lavender, thyme, lemongrass, eucalyptus, and peppermint, have been the subject of research. Even if they are not a perfect replacement for all synthetic pesticides, essential oils have the potential to be used in agricultural pest control, urban pest control, or the protection of indoor plants. They are also used in commercial insect repellents and bug spray. During testing, it was discovered that certain essential oils were just as effective as, or even more effective than, DEET, which is the most powerful insect repellent that is currently available on the market. Essential oils are only useful when they are vaporized; this is true even when they are effective as insecticides when applied topically, as in the case of a mosquito repellent. Because the vapor phase of an effective repellent only lasts for a relatively short amount of time, a mixture of polymers and cream is used to make it last longer. The use of essential oils rather than synthetic insecticides as green pesticides has environmental benefits in any form, including a reduction in the amount of residual activity. In addition, as the market for essential oils continues to grow and their popularity continues to rise among farmers who produce organic food and consumers who are environmentally conscious, an increased application of essential oils as a form of pest management may have positive implications for the environment as well as for the economy.

Various Other Applications

Essential oils have many applications besides aromatherapy, which is just one of those applications.

A lot of people use them to give things like washing a clean scent or to give their homes a pleasant aroma.

As a natural scent, they are also utilized in do-it-yourself cosmetics as well as high-quality natural products.

On top of that, essential oils have been proposed as a natural, non-hazardous alternative to man-made insect repellents such as DEET. However, the data about their effectiveness have been contradictory so far.

Studies have shown that some essential oils, such as citronella, can deter mosquitoes for up to two hours. Nevertheless, when paired with vanillin, the protection

time can be extended to a maximum of three hours.
In addition, the properties of essential oils imply that
certain of them could be utilized in an industrial context
to extend the period of time that foods can be stored
without spoiling.

3.2 Side Effects

The fact that something is found in its natural state does
not automatically render it risk-free.

Essential oils, in the same way as plants and other
herbal products do, contain a variety of bioactive
components that may be harmful to your health. On the
other hand, when essential oils are inhaled or combined
with a carrier oil before being applied to the skin, it is
generally agreed that they do not pose any health risks.
Bear in mind, however, that persons in your immediate
area, such as youngsters, pregnant women, and pets,
may inhale the stench. Keep this in mind. Nevertheless,
they could have certain unfavorable effects, such as

Rashes

Attack of asthma

Headaches

Reactions that are allergenic

Some essential oils include impurities and pollutants that could be harmful to an expecting woman's health. There are several essential oils that can be safely used during pregnancy; however, the quality as well as the brand must be evaluated. Women who are pregnant and sensitive to particular odors may be more likely to have adverse side effects from the ingestion of essential oils, including headaches, dizziness, and nausea. When essential oils are taken, they have the potential to cause discomfort and nausea, which is prevalent in pregnant women because of their heightened sensitivity to smells and tastes. Always consult a qualified medical professional before to use. Essential oils are known to cause a variety of unpleasant effects, the most common of which is a rash. However, essential oils are also capable of causing more severe reactions, and at least one person's death has been linked to the use of essential oils. Lavender, peppermint, tea tree, and ylang-ylang are the essential oils that are most commonly associated with adverse responses. Cinnamon oil, which has a high concentration of phenols, is known to aggravate skin conditions and should never be applied directly to the skin without first being combined with a carrier oil. Citrus essential oils, on the other hand, make the skin more photosensitive, which in turn raises the chance of being sunburned. It is not recommended to try to ingest essential oils because doing so can be dangerous and, in some instances, even fatal. Additionally, the safety of these oils for pregnant women and breastfeeding mothers has been the subject of very few research; as a result, pregnant women and nursing mothers are often advised to avoid using these oils. It is commonly believed that essential oils pose no health risks. However, they may have an adverse effect on certain individuals if they are ingested or applied topically to the skin in this manner. Essential oils, when combined with a base oil, are widely regarded as being safe to breathe in or apply to the skin. Nevertheless, they should not be consumed in any way. On the other hand, taking essential oils as a dietary supplement for very minor health complaints is probably safe to do. On the other hand, many of the purported health benefits connected to these foods are not supported by sufficient research, and the claims made about their effectiveness are typically exaggerated. If you have a serious medical condition or are currently on antibiotics, you should consult your primary care physician before using these products.

Chapter 4

The Native Americans' Widespread Reliance on Essential Oils for the Treatment of Ailments

The bark, resin, spices, herbs, stem, wood, seeds, kernels, flowers, and other parts of a plant can all be used to extract essential oils, also known as plant oils. Essential oils act as a sort of immune system for plants, warding off any and all diseases that may befall them. They are referred to as the "life-blood" of plants. They offer the same level of protection to humans when removed and employed in other ways. Aromatherapy makes use of essential oils, which often have a potent odor and are inhaled in order to be absorbed by the body. When used topically for massaging or for a variety of other purposes, they are sometimes mixed with base or carrier oils.

4.1 The following is a list of well-known essential oils that were utilized by native Americans.

Essential oils are extremely concentrated extracts of several plants. Aromatherapy and naturopathy are two examples of natural and alternative medicinal practices that make use of these ingredients. Numerous plant species contain compounds that might have some useful applications. However, there is typically not enough evidence to support its usage as a treatment or a cure for a variety of conditions. Essential oils may or may not be beneficial to the user, depending on the intended purpose of their use.

There is a wide range of flora that has the potential to contain active compounds. The producers have turned hundreds of these plant oils into essential oil products. Essential oils are used in aromatherapy. In spite of the fact that these oils have been used throughout history as food preservatives, the Food and Drug Administration (FDA) just recently confirmed that these oils are Generally Recognized as Safe (GRAS). The following essential oils are some of the most well-known in the world:

Eucalyptus

Orange

Chamomile

Ylang-ylangLavenderPeppermint

Tea tree

Lemon

Sweet orange

Ginger

These oils include chemicals that may have health implications for humans are following.

Headaches

Constipation

Depression

Sores from the cold

Inflammation of the sinuses

Muscle pain anxiety

4.2 The Applications of Native American Essential Oils and the Benefits They Offer

The locals do not adhere to any particular formula, with the exception of the smoking ceremony, which involves the use of smudging sticks. Instead, the Native Americans roll bundles of sage sticks into sticks to use as smudge in ceremonies. In addition, sage is widely used as an incense, and it can be purchased in stick form. The aroma of sage has a cleansing effect on the environment, removing any negative energy that may be there. Additionally, sweetgrass is utilized by Native Americans both as a herb and an oil. They have faith that sweetgrass can deodorize an area while also making it smell nice. Sweetgrass, in contrast to smudging sticks, is typically braided into a braid that is 12 inches thick. Native Americans make use of a wide variety of other herbs and oils, the majority of which are burned without the addition of any synthetics. Hydrosols can also be made from herbs such as sweetgrass, sage, juniper, and many more. This not only reduces the expense, but it also diminishes the potency of the aroma. On the other hand, any further synthetic additives to these kinds of hydrosols has to be looked at.

Basil Essential Oil

In aromatherapy, it is used to alleviate or eradicate headaches, weariness, depression, and the discomforts of asthma. Additionally, it is used to promote psychological perseverance.

It is also supposed to benefit people who have problems paying attention, allergies, congestion in the sinuses or infections, as well as fever symptoms.

The fragrance of sweet basil drives away insects and destroys bacteria that are the source of odors, making it an effective deodorizer for musty interior settings such as cars and for items such as furniture that give off an offensive odor.

Its effects on digestion help alleviate symptoms of metabolic irregularities such as nausea, hiccups, vomiting, and constipation, which can all cause discomfort.

The essential oil of basil helps to expel intestinal gas that may be caused by poor digestion or constipation.

When applied topically, Basil Essential Oil is supposed to revitalize, nourish, and support the healing of damaged or lackluster skin. This is because it stimulates the production of new skin cells.

It is often used to assist the skin's suppleness and resilience and to balance oil production, as well as to calm breakouts of acne, reduce dryness, ease symptoms of skin infections, and treat other topical illnesses.

It is said that when it is used in a diluted form, it can give exfoliating and toning capabilities, which involve the removal of dead skin as well as the balancing of skin tone to promote the complexion's natural brightness.

Bergamot Essential Oil

Bergamot Oil has antimicrobial properties that can prevent the growth of bacteria and other germs that are harmful to the skin. When it is added to bathwater or soaps, it not only protects the skin from infections but also heals skin cracks and heels.

When incorporated into hair care products, it helps to increase the shine of hair and prevents hair loss.

The sensation of pain that is caused by headaches, muscle aches, and sprains can be alleviated by using this remedy.

Bergamot Oil has cicatrizing properties, which means it can help control oil production in the skin and even out skin tone. This, in turn, helps to reduce the visibility of unattractive blemishes and scars.

When used as a natural deodorant, bergamot oil can be beneficial in its ability to eliminate the germs that cause body odor.

Fights off illnesses that are the underlying cause of fever and so contributes to the body's recuperation.

It does this while also increasing sweat, which in turn lowers the body temperature and helps the body rid itself of toxins through the skin's pores and glands.

Bergamot Oil is well-known for possessing characteristics that promote the speedy healing of wounds and eczema by preventing the wounds from becoming septic and lowering the risk of developing new infections.

Frankincense Essential Oil

It is cleansing to the soul.

A feeling of enlightenment is heightened as a result.

Increases one's awareness of, and connection to, a higher level of spiritual self or consciousness

Encourages feelings of mental equilibrium, a sense of grounding, as well as receptivity to new experiences and ideas

Reduces inflammation, discomfort, nasal congestion, and tension, all of which are potential distractions while meditation.

Myrrh Essential Oil

The cellular memory of the body can be cleared of any unfavorable thoughts or feelings.

Encourages feelings of relaxation and tranquility, which in turn lowers stress levels, boosts mental concentration, and promotes spiritual development.

Sandalwood Essential Oil

Aids in the healing of emotional and spiritual wounds.

Encourages emotional openness and builds trustworthiness.

Supports a sense of rootedness.

Removes bad thoughts and feelings from the head, improving mental clarity.

Inner noise/mental chatter is quieted, allowing you to focus on breathing.

Promotes the sensation of a calm, at-ease physique.

Restful environment

Enhances alertness

Neroli Essential Oil

Self-acceptance, courage, self-love, and personal responsibility are encouraged.

Encourages the flow of ideas

Encourages you to pursue spirituality regularly.

Mind and body are brought into balance.

Enhances mental clarity, mindfulness, and feelings of satisfaction and peace.

Reduces melancholy, tension, discomfort, and inflammation, all of which can distract during meditation and interfere with getting a good night's sleep.

Lavender Essential Oil

Relaxation, mental stability, and mental clarity are all benefits.

Encourages comfortable and restorative sleep.

Anxiety, depression, restlessness, and overall emotional instability are all reduced.

Encourages concentration and a sense of enlightenment.

Ylang Ylang Essential Oil

It has a lot of calming and relaxing characteristics.

Stress, grief, anger, impatience, and nervous tension are among the negative emotions that can be released.

Improves one's mood

Thyme Essential Oil

When used in aromatherapy, thyme oil is a tonic that has a strengthening affect on both the body and the mind.

Inhaling its stimulating smell might assist you in overcoming negative emotions such as tension, weariness, fear, and grief.

Acquiring confidence, perspective, and self-esteem, as well as a feeling of bravery when faced with periods of uncertainty or decision-making, are all good to a person's mental health and well-being.

In addition to these benefits, it is supposed to improve sleep quality, guard against seasonal illnesses such as the flu, and alleviate headaches and other body tensions.

When used directly or included in a cosmetic product, thyme oil is beneficial for individuals who have oily skin or acne.

Its antibacterial properties aid in the cleansing of the skin, the decrease of concerns related to the skin's texture, and the achievement of a complexion that is more even and radiant.

It is possible to use thyme oil in natural therapies in order to hasten the healing process of minor wounds, scrapes, sunburns, and skin infections, as well as to help control minor cases of inflammatory skin illnesses such as dermatitis and eczema. Thyme oil can be purchased online.

It is also believed that thyme oil can protect the skin against the harmful effects of the environment, such as the oxidative effects of UVA and UVB radiation that are generated by exposure to the sun. It appears from this that Thyme Oil could also be effective in anti-aging skincare products.

The medical benefits of thyme oil have been applied to a wide variety of conditions, ranging from wounds and infections to high blood pressure.

It is believed that it acts as a stimulant to all of the body's systems, so encouraging the efficient and healthy functioning of the body's biological processes.

It is also stated that taking thyme oil might improve overall health and well-being by strengthening the immune system.

It acts as a carminative, aids in the decrease of bloating, and assists in the digesting process.

Because of its warming and calming nature, thyme oil can be used as a natural pain therapy for people who are suffering from physical exhaustion as well as muscular discomfort, strain, and stiffness.

Particularly, the expectorant characteristics of Thyme Oil assist in the expansion of airways, the relief of minor respiratory irritation, and the suppression of coughs.

Sage Essential Oil

Eliminate all forms of impure energy from the mind, body, and spiritual areas in order to achieve purity.

Restores fading energy.

The mind and spirit are both stimulated and refined while also being grounded.

Raise(s) one's level of happiness.

Enhances emotional stability.

Provides solace and enhancement of perception, which assists in the reduction of unfavorable feelings such as fatigue.

Improves the ability to retain memories and fosters a sense of focus.

The discomforts in the respiratory system are alleviated.

Cinnamon Bark Essential Oil

The oil is beneficial to both the skin and the hair, and it is well-known for the high level of antioxidants that it contains.

It is regarded to be soothing to the skin when used topically as part of a cosmetic formulation.

Its natural astringent properties help in cleansing and toning the skin, which gives it the appearance of being taut and full of vitality.

Additionally, it helps to minimize the appearance of wrinkles, age spots, and fine lines while also balancing complexions to give the appearance of a more youthful appearance.

It is an ingredient in a natural face cleanser that is used to clean the face. in order to minimize the appearance of pores, tame excess oil production, and supply calming moisture.

When used in hair care products, cinnamon bark oil helps to remove buildup from the scalp while also producing healthier-looking, fuller-looking hair.

The aromatic quality of natural perfumes can be improved with the use of the oil.

Vetiver Essential Oil

When practicing mindfulness practices, it helps with attention by putting the mind at ease and preventing it from straying.

Produces a sedative and tranquilizing effect on the mind as well as the body.

There is treatment for the symptoms of insomnia.

It helps bring one's spirit back down to earth.

The state of mind is made more calm and peaceful as a means of improving one's ability to concentrate on something.

When done at the end of a long day, it helps the mind and body wind down and relax.

Anxiety, weariness, and feelings of anger, despair, fear, and insecurity are all reduced as a result of this medication's effects.

Palo Santo Essential Oil

Native Americans hold this tree in high regard as a sacred being.

Fosters a sense of steadiness and tranquillity in its surroundings.

It gets rid of unpleasant feelings and concepts.

A place of meditation allows for the release of negative energy.

Cedarwood Atlas Essential Oil

You are encouraged to concentrate on your higher self by gazing within, which is especially helpful when your attention is being divided.

It can help people get back on track with their spiritual journey when they feel as though they have hit a roadblock.

It protects against energy that is negative.

It has a calming and reassuring effect, both on the mind and on the spirit.

Chamomile Essential Oils

There is a decrease in inflammation, as well as discomfort, spasms, and tension.

The calming effect encourages comfortable sleep and alleviates painful joint inflammation.

Promotes the overall health of the skin

Rosemary Essential Oil

Increases attentiveness and stimulates circulation.

Enhances attention by reviving the senses and promoting mental clarity.

Headaches are relieved.

Lemon Essential Oil

Improves one's mood.

Energizes the mind and refreshes the skin.

When you're feeling lethargic, it might help you feel more optimistic, confident, and secure. It can also help you feel more determined.

Essential Oil Of Orange (Sweet)

Eases feelings of stress and negative emotions, such as anxiety, by uplifting the mood, energizing the mind, and increasing attentiveness.

Ginger Essential Oil

Reduces the feeling of nausea and the likelihood of vomiting.

Physical aches and pains are relieved.

Mentally and physically stimulating

Reduces tiredness

Comforts during Cold and Flu

Cardamom Essential Oil

Reduces the feeling of nausea and the likelihood of vomiting.

Physical aches and pains are relieved.

Mentally and physically stimulating

Black Pepper Essential Oil

Mentally and physically stimulating

Reduces the intensity of nausea as well as the possibility of throwing up.

The patient feels relief from their aches and pains physically.

Mental and physical stimulation combined.

Helps one feel less weary.

Relievers during Episodes of the Cold and Flu

Encourages a sense of rootedness.

Marjoram Essential Oil

All of the symptoms of bloating, flatulence, cramping, and constipation are alleviated.

Provides assistance to the digestive system.

The discomfort, spasms, and nausea are all alleviated.

It is good for the circulation.

Cypress Essential Oil

Relaxation is facilitated by the sedative property.

There is an increase in clarity and concentration.

Raise(s) one's level of happiness.

Induces feelings of calm and a sense of being firmly established in one's place.

Makes it possible to breathe more easily.

Relaxes spasms.

Essential Oil Of Helichrysum

Inflammation, discomfort, and muscular spasms are reduced.

Immune and intestinal health is aided.

Improves sleep quality

Cramps and bloating are relieved.

Improves the appearance of skin that is prone to blemishes.

Essential Oil Of Peppermint

It has a cooling effect on the skin, which relieves muscle pain and tension.

Comforts blocked nose and congested chest due to cold

Inflammation, soreness, and spasms are reduced.

Improves concentration

Have the ability to both warm and cool

Itching, inflammation, sunburn, and muscle aches can all be relieved with this product.

Skin softening

Assistance in the treatment of oily hair and skin

Headache relief

Mild coughing relief

The mind's concentration

Enhance memory

Eucalyptus Essential Oil

Inflammation and pain are reduced.

Reduces tiredness and fatigue.

Relieves mental fatigue and headaches.

Boosts a weakened immune system.

It improves mental clarity.

Tea Tree Essential Oil

Pinene, Sabinene, Myrcene, -Phellandrene, p-Cymene, Terpinolene, Terpinene, Limonene, Linalool, 1, 8-cineole, gamma-Terpinene, Terpinene-4-ol, and Terpineol are the primary ingredients of Tea Tree Oil.

Tea Tree Essential Oil is a type of essential oil used to treat a variety of illnesses. Its characteristics include anti-inflammatory, analgesic, antimicrobial, sedative, anti-mutagenic, antiviral, antibacterial, antifungal, and antispasmodic.

Immune system booster

Its antibacterial capabilities are a plus.

On touch, reduce or eliminate dangerous microorganisms and diseases.

It is used to treat rashes, burns, dandruff, acne, Athlete's Foot, and head lice, among other things.

Use on wounds because of its anti-inflammatory, expectorant, antibacterial, and bronchodilator effects.

Sabinene is thought to function as an antioxidant with antibacterial and antifungal effects.

It can also be used to treat skin irritation.

It is thought to improve cerebral blood flow, relieve tension headaches, and suppress coughing.

to aid in the reduction of stress, the treatment of depression, and the relief of inflammation

Tea Tree Oil is found in laundry soaps, polishes, hand soaps, air fresheners, and insect repellents, among other things.

It kills mold and hazardous bacteria on surfaces like shower curtains and dishwashers, and it works the same way in the air when dispersed.

This oil's fresh, slightly medicinal, camphor-like perfume has been compared to that of the Eucalyptus plant, and it has been shown to alleviate brain fog, weariness, and stress when used for aromatherapy.

Tea Tree Oil is a good ingredient for personal hygiene cosmetic items and toiletries such as bar shampoos, massage oils, conditioners, deodorants, salves, soaps, face washes, body washes, moisturizers, and nail conditioners when used topically and cosmetically.

Grapefruit Essential Oil

Inflammation is reduced.

It can help to lift one's spirits.

When the mind is stressed, it refreshes and comforts it.

Encourages a feeling of calm, contentment, and optimism.

Immune function is improved.

Headaches are relieved.

When you're feeling tired, this supplement can help you feel more energized.

Enhances mental insight and clarity.

Chapter 5

Native Americans Essential Oils—Recipes to Cure Illness

Essential oils can be utilized for a variety of things, from stress relief to infection protection on the skin.

Stress Relief Massage Blend With Lavender

Ingredients:

7 teaspoons Carrier Oil (Avocado, Sweet Almond, or Grape Seed suggested)

4 drops Mandarin Essential Oil

4 drops Lavender Essential Oil

5 drops Bergamot Essential Oil

3 drops Lemongrass Essential Oil

Instructions:

In a dark glass or plastic bottle, combine the essential oils.

Add the carrier oil to dilute the combination.

Massage onto the chest for soothing, deep warmth.

Ingredients:

60 ml (2 oz.) Sage Oil

30 ml (1 oz.) Coconut Carrier Oil

Carrie, jojoba, jojoba, jojoba,

Chapter 6

Native Americans Essential Oils - Recipes to Cure Illness

I ntroduction

The passage of time and the development of the world have resulted in a considerable growth in the quantity of technology, which has both simplified life and made it significantly more difficult. This is a consequence of the fact that the amount of technology has significantly increased. The human body has been weakened as a result of irregular eating and sleeping routines, as well as a stressful life, because the accumulation of material possessions has become the primary goal of human existence. As a direct consequence of this development, the conflict has become more intense.

We are ignoring the demands of our body as well as our health in order to put all of our attention and energy into accomplishing our goals and becoming successful. This is because our day-to-day lives are so chaotic. Our way of life, including the food that we eat, has become increasingly disconnected from the natural world. People's eating habits have shifted in response to the large amount of work that needs to be done, and the shift has been toward putting more of an emphasis on manufactured foodstuff that is easily accessible. This has had a tremendous influence on human health since it has steadily weakened the immune system. As a direct consequence of this, we are now more likely to suffer from a variety of diseases. Then, for the aim of receiving treatment, we would engage in a variety of various sorts of therapy and make use of a wide range of different pharmaceuticals.

Each and every one of the chemicals that we put into our bodies in the form of medication has its own effect on the human body, and just like any other factor, that effect could either be good or detrimental to our health, depending on the circumstances. Things that are organic and natural have an influence on the human body that is both less damaging and more beneficial than other effects. It is essential that we incorporate them into our daily lives and make them a regular part of our diets if we want to have a stronger immune system.

When it comes to treating common disorders, a well-known authority on health explains to Govindan that using home remedies rather than over-the-counter medications is preferable. This is due to the fact that OTC pills can have undesirable side effects."

For instance, the antihistamine Aleve has been shown to cause agitation and hyperactivity in certain people. When taking this type of medication, it can be difficult for some people to get to sleep or keep from waking up during the night." In any event, they all recommend scheduling an appointment with your primary care physician if you notice that your condition is affecting your ability to carry out normal activities of daily living.

When it comes to treating any kind of illness, the greatest method that has always been to use home remedies that consist of natural and healthy ingredients has always been the best course of action. This is especially important to keep in mind when administering medical care to children, who, in comparison to adults, have a more delicate constitution and a less robust immune system. It is always advisable to treat their sickness with natural remedies as opposed to presenting them with more artificial cures or harsh pharmaceuticals, both of which have the potential to leave some detrimental impacts on both their physical and mental health.

The vast majority of respondents to our study voiced an interest in exploring the possibility of treating common health problems with natural therapies first, with the goal of avoiding the necessity of resorting to the use of pharmaceutical pharmaceuticals. A previous history of positive experiences with the treatment, as well as the alleviation of symptoms, are also additional factors that contribute to the utilization of home remedies.

This book is stuffed to the brim with great knowledge on the natural healthy sicknesses that are highly valuable for the human body, and it also has some helpful information regarding some mental and physical ailments children could have and suffer a lot from. Your child's physical well-being is essential to his or her ability to meet the difficulties of today's fast-paced living and achieve success in this world. The home remedies that are discussed in the guide constitute the answer to these issues, which may be found in their entirety within the handbook. Your child will be able to get better and have a healthy body by using these home remedies, which will help your child recover from the troubles they are having.

On this large piece of land, we have diverse regions that are endowed with a range of remarkable types of natural capital. These kinds of natural capital are unique to that location. The diets of the people who reside in that particular region are affected by the fact that they raise their own crops and animals due to the fact that they do so themselves. They incorporate foods made from these natural resources into their diets and also use them for a variety of medicinal purposes, which they incorporate into their everyday life.

The types of soil, minerals, and water that are present in a given place determine the kinds of natural resources that may be found on each continent, including Europe, Asia, Africa, and America. These natural resources are what give each continent its own distinctive set of natural resources. Every nation puts in labor on the land with the support of these components, and cultivates the land with nutritious foods for the people to consume and draw benefits from, so that they may have a decent bodily and mental state. It is and has always been a good practice to give such natural food to children so that they can develop in a better manner and have a healthy physique. This is because children can develop in a better manner when they have a healthy physique. This is due to the fact that organic medicines do provide a wide variety of potential business prospects. Indigenous peoples have been cultivating the land in what is now known as North America for thousands upon thousands of years. As a direct result of the region's varied and abundant soil, the locals were in a position to supply for not just their own families but also for the community as a whole. The abundant and nutrient-dense crops that are native to the Americas can today be farmed on practically every continent, making them available for use in a broad variety of cuisines and contributing to the feeding of the world.

Chapter 7

Native American foods

For thousands of years, the land that is now known as North America was cultivated by indigenous peoples. The fertile and varied soil of the region enabled the indigenous people of the area to provide food for their family and the communities in which they lived. The abundant and nutritious crops that are native to the Americas are now grown on practically every continent, making them available to a wide range of cuisines and helping to ensure that the globe never goes hungry.

Here are some foods that are indigenous to the Americas; you can get many of them at our local farmer's markets during the fall and into the winter. As we gather around our dinner tables to celebrate the holiday season, let us not forget that the land on which we currently reside in the Bay Area was historically and illegally taken from the Ohlone people. Let us respect the natural bounty of our region as well as the expertise and hard work put in by the native populations in order to care for the land and tend to these crops.

1.1 What kinds of meals are typical in Native American cuisine?

Corn, often known as Indian corn, was the most important food crop for Native Americans (also called as maize, which drives from the Taino Indian name for the plant.) Maize was cultivated by the majority of American and Indian tribes; even members of tribes that did not grow their own corn sometimes bartered for it with members of other nearby tribes. Among the most important crops cultivated by American Indians were beans, avocados, squash, pumpkins, wild rice, tomatoes, sweet potatoes, papayas, peanuts, peppers, sunflowers, and chocolate.

Even though they did not practice agriculture, the majority of Native American tribes consumed a significant amount of meat in their diet. It was common to eat meat from buffalo, caribou, elk, deer, and rabbit. Salmon and other fish, turkeys, ducks, geese, and other birds, clams and other shellfish, and marine animals like as seals and whales were also consumed. However, almost every species that resided in the Americas during the ancient times was occasionally added to the menu. This included animals like porcupines, monkeys, and snakes that you might not think of as food. Because the majority of Native American tribes adhered to the principle of not wasting food, they would frequently make an effort to consume any animal that had been killed for another purpose.

Eggs, maple syrup, honey, and sugar, nuts, salt (including cashews, peanuts, hickory nuts, pine nuts, and acorns), fruit (including cranberries, wild plums, blueberries, chokecherries, strawberries, persimmons, and raspberries), and a wide variety of beans, roots, and greens were all naturally found in the Americas and were commonly consumed by American Indians.

1.2 How would you describe the Native American meal courses as a whole?

The process of cooking in Native American culture was typically very uncomplicated. The vast majority of Native Americans favored eating their food uncooked and with very minimal seasonings or spices. The Indians who lived in Mexico and Central America, on the other hand, preferred to reduce the amount of fresh meat they used in their cooking and increase the amount of spices and flavorings such as chili peppers, cumin, and chocolate. Historically, meat was grilled over hot stones or roasted over an open fire. It was common practice to smoke or bake the fish. A number of indigenous communities favored stews and soups. Corn was ingested in a variety of forms, including on the cob, popcorn, hominy, tortillas, and corn bread baked in clay ovens. These forms were all common ways of consuming corn. Desserts such as fruit puddings and maple sweets were favorites in a number of different cultures. Although the vast majority of indigenous people in North America drank water with their meals, Mexicans enjoyed drinking hot chocolate, and indigenous people in other parts of South and Central America created chicha, an alcoholic beverage made from corn.

Squash, winter

Even before the Mayflower set foot on Plymouth Rock, Native Americans were cultivating a number of different winter squash varieties for harvest. Winter squash is one of our favorite fall symbols. The early colonists relied heavily on gourds, pumpkins, and squash for both food and medical purposes. These vegetables are all members of the Cucurbita family. The distinction between winter squash and summer squash dates back to a time when seasonality had a larger role in people's ability to survive. When the skin of winter squash begins to harden in the fall, it is then possible to harvest the squash and store it away until spring, allowing it to survive the colder months. There is now a variety of winter squash accessible throughout the year in a wide range of colors, sizes, and flavors. The most well-known varieties of winter squash are butternut, spaghetti, and acorn, but local farmers are helping us learn about other members of the winter squash family that are less well-known. These farmers are bringing charming sweet dumpling squash and warty heirloom Galeux D'Eysines to market.

Corn

Corn is a plant that is native to the United States and is thought to have originated in Mexico or Central America. Corn has played and will continue to play a significant role in the continued existence of many native communities. It has been put to use for a wide variety of things, including the provision of food, shelter, and fuel. Corn is referred to as Zea mays on a scientific level. This is the conventional name for corn, which is more commonly known as maize and is utilized in a lot of different places around the world.

In addition to the yellow and white sweet varieties, flour corn can also be found in a range of other colors, including red, blue, pink, and black. Because heat and/or direct sunlight rapidly convert the sugars in corn kernels into starch, sweet corn should only be purchased from stores that have been stored at a cool temperature or in the shade. Look for ears of corn that still have their husks green and are not stale. They should wrap the ear entirely and not be too loose in the slightest. To check the kernels, pull back a portion of the husk and look at them closely; they should be full and neatly spaced in rows. Corn can be stored in a plastic bag in the refrigerator for up to three days; however, the flavor will be better preserved if the husk is left on.

Fresh corn has a relatively brief growing season in the Bay Area. Before freezing the cob or the kernels to use at a later time in the year, blanch them for about five minutes. In order to avoid the husk from catching fire while the corn is being grilled or broiled, it should be soaked in water beforehand.

Corn, which was traditionally referred to as "the maize," was domesticated 10,000 years ago in what is now Mexico by Olmec and Mayan people. It is regarded to be one of the oldest domesticated crops in existence. Corn is the name that English immigrants gave to the crop, and it quickly became an important source of food for them due to the fact that it could be preserved or consumed fresh. Corn was given the name corn by English immigrants. Nixtamalization is a process that was developed by early Mesoamerican societies to manufacture masa from corn. Masa is a type of flour that is used in making tortillas, tamales, and other meals that are consumed throughout the year.

Avocados

People who were indigenous to Mexico and Central America cultivated avocado trees and held the fruit in high regard for millennia before it became trendy to spread avocado on toast. The Maya even used a representation of an avocado as a symbol to indicate the 14th month of the year on their calendar. At the moment, the state of California produces the most avocados of any other state in the United States.

Peppers, chile

The latter part of summer is when chili peppers have the most intense flavor. Capsaicin, the chemical compound that gives hot peppers their characteristic spiciness, cannot be produced without a protracted and warm phase of growth. The production of capsaicin is a trait that most likely developed in order to discourage mammalian consumption of the fruit. Birds, who are drawn to the vivid colors of peppers despite being unfazed by their heat, are responsible for the wild distribution of their seeds. We humans appreciate the pungency of the chile, despite the peppery attempts of the chilli to deter us from eating it. In point of fact, we've established ourselves as highly successful wholesalers of pepper seed. It is believed that peppers were one of the first plants to be tamed and domesticated in the Americas thousands of years ago. After bringing back pepper seeds from his first trip to Spain, Christopher Columbus helped spread the crop over Europe, Southeast Asia, and India after discovering the pepper. Today, peppers are incorporated into the cuisines of many different nations in a wide range of different ways. Chile powder is one of the spices that is used all over the world the most frequently. Scoville heat units are a measurement of how spicy a pepper is. These units were named after the person who developed a method to determine the amount of capsaicin in a pepper. 0 on the scale, with jalapenos coming in at 5,000 and habaneros coming in about 500,000. The capsaicinoid molecule that makes up pepper spray has a rating of 5,000,000 units, and it is the active element in the product. Although peppers with lower Scoville ratings are more widespread in the United States than their more fiery counterparts, it appears that spicier peppers are becoming increasingly popular in our country's culinary traditions.

Potatoes

Despite the fact that potatoes are sometimes misidentified as an Irish crop, those who "discovered" America brought this starchy vegetable back with them to Europe following their travels. Potatoes are believed to have originated in the Andes region of South America some 1,800 years ago. At that time, the Inca people were the first known people to cultivate them. More than a thousand different varieties of potatoes are currently cultivated, with Chile being responsible for more than 99 percent of these variations.

Dried beans

One of the earliest domesticated plant species was the Fabaceae family, which includes the bean. They only come in second place to cereals in terms of providing the world's population with calories and protein, but they have two to four times the amount of protein that grains do. It is possible to obtain a complete protein by combining grains and beans in the same meal. The consumption of beans can result in a variety of positive health effects, such as a lower cholesterol level, more stable blood sugar levels, and protection against cancer. They have a high fiber content, which means that eating them makes you feel satiated for a longer period of time.

Beans, both fresh and dried, can be purchased in the farmers market; however, fresh beans can only be obtained during the months of summer and fall. A common food staple, dried beans have a longer shelf life than their fresh counterparts, making them available throughout the year. When compared to boiling beans from dried stock, buying canned beans is not only more expensive but also less healthful. Beans that have been canned are often heavy in sodium and other preservatives, and the majority of cans are lined with BPA, a chemical that has been linked to cancer and hormone disruption.

Beans are known to generate flatulence because of the presence of oligosaccharides in them. These oligosaccharides, when metabolized by bacteria in the colon, release carbon dioxide. Adding spices like ginger, turmeric, and asafetida to the mixture, as well as soaking beans for an entire night, is proven to be beneficial. Additionally, sprouting beans makes digestion and absorption much simpler processes. After removing the beans from the soaking liquid, they should be washed thoroughly with fresh water. Once the water and beans have reached a light boil, reduce the heat to a low setting and continue to cook for around twenty minutes, or until the beans are tender. The type of bean determines both the quantity of water and the amount of time necessary to complete the cooking process. When the beans are being cooked, the addition of salty or acidic items like vinegar, tomatoes, or lime might cause them to become tough and extend the amount of time needed to boil them. When cooking beans, B vitamins and folic acid are lost, so it is important to save the liquid that the beans are cooked in.

Tomatoes

Tomatoes, which are frequently associated with the cuisine of Italy, really originated in South and Central

America and were first domesticated in Mexico by the native people of that country. Cooking with tomatoes was a common practice among the Aztecs long before the arrival of the Spanish (who subsequently exported the tomato to Europe). Aztecs cultivated both green tomatoes, known as tomatl in Nahuatl, sometimes known as tomatillos, and red tomatoes, known as xictomatl, and used them in a wide variety of culinary preparations.

Tomatillos

If you like green salsa, you ought to get knowledgeable about tomatillos. Tomatillos were first domesticated by the Aztecs around 800 BC and have since become an essential ingredient in Mexican cuisine. Tomatillos date back to that time period. The fruit of the tomatillo, which is known as "tomate verde" in Mexico, is resolutely green, roughly the size of a large cherry, and contains more flesh than a tomato does. They attain maturity concealed under a papery husk of a light brown color. The husk is a wonderful indicator of freshness; however, because it is inedible, it must be removed before the product can be used. The tomatillo fruit can be utilized as a foundation for chile sauces, which are typically referred to as salsa verde (green sauce). This will help to moderate the heat of the pepper while simultaneously boosting your appetite. Because of the acidic flavor that tomatillos have, they can be cooked, eaten raw, chopped, or blended to complement many ready-made foods. Guacamole and tortilla soup are two additional dishes that go wonderfully with tomatillos.

Sweet potatoes

According to legend, this well-known tuber can trace its roots back to either Central or South America. As early as 5,000 years ago, it was domesticated in Central America, and as early as 1,000 years ago, it was domesticated in parts of Polynesia. Because of their susceptibility to damage from both freezing temperatures and drought, sweet potatoes are best grown in warm, tropical areas. The sweet potato root can be harvested anywhere from two to nine months after planting, depending on the cultivar (there are over 400 types). Because they are grown from cuttings taken from the vine rather than seeds, cultivation is simplified.

Sweet potatoes provide abundant amounts of dietary fiber, beta-carotene, complex carbohydrates, and a variety of other vitamins and nutrients. They can have beige, orange, red, or purple flesh, and their color can range from beige to orange to red to purple. In North America, the popular orange-fleshed variety of the sweet potato that is referred to as a "yam" is actually a sweet potato. (Botanically speaking, sweet potatoes and yams are two separate species.) Yams belong to the family Dioscoreaceae, whereas sweet potatoes are a member of the Convolvulaceae (bindweed) family.

Although North Carolina is the leading producer of sweet potatoes in the United States (with California, Mississippi, and Louisiana all fighting for second place), China is the leading grower of sweet potatoes on a global scale. Although most people are familiar with the root of the sweet potato, its leaves and shoots also have a delicious flavor. In Korean cuisine, sweet potato starch is utilized in the production of cellophane noodles, and in South American cooking, red sweet potatoes are combined with lime juice to produce a fabric dye.

CPSIA information can be obtained
at www.ICGtesting.com
Printed in the USA
BVHW070530140123
656277BV00014B/1177